The Word Wizard's Book of HOMONYMS

Robin Johnson

Crabtree
Publishing
Company
www.crabtreebooks.com

Word Wizard

Author
Robin Johnson

Publishing plan research and development
Reagan Miller

Editorial director
Kathy Middleton

Project coordinator
Kelly Spence

Editor
Anastasia Suen

Proofreader and indexer
Wendy Scavuzzo

Photo research
Robin Johnson, Katherine Berti

Design & prepress
Katherine Berti

Print coordinator
Katherine Berti

Photographs
Thinkstock: cover (bottom right)
All other images from Shutterstock

Library and Archives Canada Cataloguing in Publication

Johnson, Robin (Robin R.), author
    The word wizard's book of homonyms / Robin Johnson.

(Word wizard)
Includes index.
Issued in print and electronic formats.
ISBN 978-0-7787-1920-5 (bound).--ISBN 978-0-7787-1924-3 (pbk.).--
ISBN 978-1-4271-7792-6 (pdf).--ISBN 978-1-4271-7788-9 (html)

    1. English language--Homonyms--Juvenile literature. I. Title.

PE1595.J64 2015   j428.1   C2014-907797-1
                                         C2014-907798-X

Library of Congress Cataloging-in-Publication Data

Johnson, Robin (Robin R.) author.
 The Word Wizard's book of homonyms / Robin Johnson.
    pages cm. -- (Word Wizard)
 Includes index.
 ISBN 978-0-7787-1920-5 (reinforced library binding) --
ISBN 978-0-7787-1924-3 (pbk.) -- ISBN 978-1-4271-7792-6 (electronic pdf) --
ISBN 978-1-4271-7788-9 (electronic html)
1. English language--Homonyms--Juvenile literature. 2. English language--
Parts of speech--Juvenile literature. 3. English language--Grammar--
Juvenile literature. 4. Language arts (Primary) 5. Language arts
(Elementary) I. Title. II. Title: Book of homonyms.

PE1595.J65 2015
421'.5--dc23
                                                         2014045067

Crabtree Publishing Company

Printed in Canada/022015/IH20141209

www.crabtreebooks.com   1-800-387-7650

Published in Canada
Crabtree Publishing
616 Welland Ave.
St. Catharines, Ontario
L2M 5V6

Published in the United States
Crabtree Publishing
PMB 59051
350 Fifth Avenue, 59th Floor
New York, New York 10118

Published in the United Kingdom
Crabtree Publishing
Maritime House
Basin Road North, Hove
BN41 1WR

Published in Australia
Crabtree Publishing
3 Charles Street
Coburg North
VIC 3058

Contents

Magical words

Words are magical! They tell twisted tales of dragon tails. They guide brave knights in dark nights. Words let you see the blue sea. They color oranges orange. They give you pairs of pears. Words help a fly fly. They make a duck duck. They cover a bare bear. Words can do anything!

Magic words can make a hare disappear. They can turn your hair into a rainbow.

Spell some spells

Magic words let you hear stories here. They help you tell stories there. We use words called **homonyms** to tell our tales. Homonyms look or sound like other words. The Word Wizards can cast magic spells. But they need your help to read and spell homonyms!

This girl read a red book high in the clouds. The wind blew her across the blue sky.

Magic words can take you anywhere! These kids have been playing in some beans.

Magic words show you how elephants pack their trunks. They help you spot the spots on giraffes.

What are homonyms?

Homonyms are words that look or sound the same but have different **meanings**. The meaning of a word is the idea it shows. Homonyms can be tricky! They make it hard to write the right words. The words "write" and "right" are homonyms. They sound the same but have different meanings. "Write" means to form letters and words. "Right" means correct or proper. It can also mean a direction.

Does this arrow point right or left? If you said right, you are right!

This boy has the right idea! He will write a big story with his big pencil.

The right stuff

Homonyms are also called **multiple-meaning words**. "Multiple" means more than one. Knowing that some words have more than one meaning helps you understand stories. It also helps you pick the right words to write your stories. Which picture on this page would you describe using the words "sun" and "son?"

Hold the homophone!

There are two kinds of homonyms. One kind is called a **homophone**. Homophones are words that sound alike but have different spellings and different meanings. We say, "The girl in the blue hat blew the loud party horn." The words "blue" and "blew" are homophones. Can you think of other homophones? You have already seen some in this book.

The blue balloon was feeling blue. Now it is happy because someone blew it up!

Word Wizard in training

Help the Word Wizard finish the **sentences** below. A sentence is a complete thought or idea. Look at the pictures. Then point to a word from the list to fill in each blank. Be careful! The words are homophones. They sound the same but mean different things.

flower   nose
be   flour
knows   bee

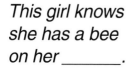

This girl knows she has a bee on her _____.

This chef has messy _____ all over her hands!

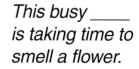

This busy _____ is taking time to smell a flower.

Too many to choose!

Some homophones have three or more meanings. That can be two meanings too many! They're hard to read and write sometimes. But there are ways to figure out their meanings.

You can try a homophone in a sentence. Then check your work by changing it to another word. If the sentence still makes sense, you used the right homophone. If it does not make sense, try again. Look at the charts on the next page. They show some common homophones and how to check them.

These kids are happy for Halloween! They're wearing their costumes here and there.

Homophone	Meaning	Example	Test	Example
there	The word "there" means in, at, or to a place.	The girl is standing over there.	Try changing the word "there" to "here."	The girl is standing over here.
their	The word "their" means belonging to people, animals, or things.	I went to their house after school.	Try changing the word "their" to "our."	I went to our house after school.
they're	The word "they're" is a **contraction**. It joins the words "they" and "are."	They're my best friends.	Try changing the word "they're" to "they are."	They are my best friends.

Homophone	Meaning	Example	Test	Example
two	The word "two" is a number.	He has two sisters.	Try changing the word "two" to a different number.	He has three sisters.
too	The word "too" can mean more than what is wanted or needed.	I have too much work to do!	Try changing the word "too" to "so."	I have so much work to do!
too	The word "too" can also mean "in addition."	I like bananas, and I like apples too.	Try changing the word "too" to "also."	I like bananas, and I like apples also.
to	The word "to" means for or moving in a direction.	She rides her bike to school.	Use the word "to" if the other homophones do not make sense.	She rides her bike ~~two too~~ to school.

These two kids are having too much fun! They're talking about homophones on their banana phones!

This boy has too many cookies to eat! If he ate all eight, he would get a tummy ache!

Spelled the same

Homographs are other kinds of homonyms. These words are spelled the same but have different meanings. Some homographs sound the same. We say, "The super kids can fly like flies!" The word "fly" is a homograph. It can mean to zoom through the air. It can also mean a pesky insect.

Word Wizard in training

The Word Wizard can fly like a fly, but she needs your help with homographs! Read the sentences below. Point to words that are spelled the same but have different meanings. What does each homograph mean? Look at the pictures for clues.

This cool superhero eats cool ice cream.

This super boy rocks! He can lift heavy rocks.

These super kids like to play in the park. Today they are putting on a play.

This super girl never dresses in dresses!

How you say it

Some homographs look the same but sound different. The way we **pronounce** them shows their meaning. To pronounce means to say a word correctly. We say, "The boy bows in karate class." The word "bows" **rhymes** with "cows" in that sentence. We say, "The girl wears bows in her hair." The word "bows" rhymes with "nose" in that sentence.

Word Wizard in training

The Word Wizard needs more help with homographs! He wants to learn how to pronounce the word "wind." It can mean to turn or wrap something around. Then it rhymes with "find." It can also mean moving air. Then it rhymes with "pinned." Decide how to pronounce "wind" in the sentences below. Then read the sentences out loud. You will blow the Word Wizard away!

The wind will carry the dandelion seeds far away.

The wind is blowing these balloons.

The robots walk and talk when you wind them up.

The girl will wind the string to bring her kite down.

Paint a picture

Homographs can make stories hard to understand. You must figure out their meanings. You can paint a picture in your mind to help you. Look at this sentence. "The girl went fishing and caught a bass." A bass can be a musical instrument. Then it rhymes with "face." It can also be a type of fish. Then it rhymes with "glass." How should we pronounce "bass" in our sentence? Which way makes sense?

There is something fishy about these pictures! If we pronounce words wrong, stories will not make sense!

Word Wizard in training

Help the Word Wizard figure out the stories below. Read the sentences carefully. Imagine both meanings of the homographs. Which meaning makes sense? Look at the pictures for clues. Then read the sentences to the Word Wizard.

The cat and dog need to close the fridge. There are people close by!

The kids present some cookies they made. The cookies are a present for Santa Claus.

Look for clues

We look for clues to understand homographs. The words around homographs can help us figure out their meanings. We say, "The girl cannot see a thing without her glasses!" Some glasses help us see. Other glasses let us drink. Which meaning makes sense in that sentence?

This girl cannot see very well without her glasses!

Word Wizard in training

The Word Wizard wants you to be a word detective! Read the sentences below. Think of two meanings for each red word. Then study the other words for clues. Which meaning makes sense? Point to the picture that shows your answer.

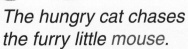

The hungry cat chases the furry little *mouse*.

The child grabs a wooden *bat* to play baseball.

The boy does not want to leave the beach. He tries to *duck* under the sand to hide!

Know your homonyms

It is important two use the write words when you right your stories. If you do knot, your tails will not make cents. Readers will not no what you mean. They will not sea the pictures ewe paint with words. Some of the words you just read are the wrong homonyms. Did you spot them? Did they make the sentences hard to understand?

Homonyms let girls with pigtails write pig tales.

Homonyms give you a hand! They help people see the sea you paint with words.

Check your spelling!

You should always check your work for spelling mistakes. If you use a computer, it can check your work for you. It will show you words that are spelled wrong. Computers cannot tell that you used the wrong words, though. Homonyms are too tricky for them. Homonyms are not too tricky for you, though! You are smarter than a computer!

Computers can help you with lots of things. But they cannot help you with homonyms!

Right on!

Now it is your turn to turn into a Word Wizard! Read the story below. Point to the right words to tell the zebra tale. You will earn your stripes. You will make magic with words. You will be a Word Wizard!

It's all black and white

One day, a zebra put on a red/read hat and went four/for a walk. It walked up a rode/road. It went hear/here. It went their/there/they're. There was just won/one problem. The zebra was not allowed/aloud to/two/too leave the zoo! People herd/heard about the zebra on the news. They red/read about the zebra in newspapers. Would/wood you read a tale/tail about a zebra in a red hat? You just did!

The zebra is black and white and red all over. A newspaper is black and white and read all over.

Learning more

Books

A Bat Cannot Bat, a Stair Cannot Stare: More about Homonyms and Homophones (Words Are CATegorical) by Brian P. Cleary. Millbrook Press, 2014.

Eight Ate: A Feast of Homonym Riddles by Marvin Terban. HMH Books for Young Readers, 2007.

Half-Pipe Homonyms (Grammar All-Stars) by Anna Prokos. Gareth Stevens Publishing, 2009.

If You Were a Homonym or a Homophone (Word Fun) by Nancy Loewen. Picture Window Books, 2007.

Websites

Help Regan the rabbit fill in the blanks in this fun brain game.
www.funbrain.com/whichword/

Hold the phone and play some homophone games at this website.
www.learninggamesforkids.com/vocabulary-games/homophones-games/homophones.html

Match up homonyms to show a hidden picture in this super Scholastic game.
www.missmaggie.org/scholastic/supermatch_eng_launcher.html

Words to know

contraction (kuhn-TRAK-shuhn) A word that combines two words using an apostrophe, such as wouldn't and can't

homograph (HOM-uh-graf) A word that is spelled the same as another word but has a different meaning

homonym (HOM-uh-nim) A word that looks or sounds like another word but has a different meaning

homophone (HOM-uh-fohn) A word that sounds like another word but is spelled differently and has a different meaning

meaning (MEE-ning) The idea that is shown by a word

multiple (MUHL-tuh-puhl) More than one

multiple-meaning word (MUHL-tuh-puhl MEE-ning wurd) Another name for a homonym

pronounce (pruh-NOUNS) To say a word correctly

rhyme (rahym) To have or end with the same sound as another word

sentence (SEN-tns) A complete thought or idea

Index